MAKING MONEY ON YOUTUBE:
ULTIMATE GUIDE

By

W. JAMES HARDING

Contents

Introduction

Welcome to "Making Money on YouTube: Ultimate Guide ". If you're a content creator on YouTube or aspiring to become one, you're in the right place. YouTube has become a global phenomenon, with billions of viewers and an ever-growing community of content creators. It's no longer just a platform for sharing videos, but also a potential source of income for those who understand the strategies and opportunities available for monetization. As a marketing expert and experienced You-Tuber, I have witnessed the evolution of YouTube as a powerful platform for content creators to turn their passion into profit. Through trial and error, I have learned the ins and outs of making money on YouTube and have successfully implemented various strategies to monetize my own channel. In this book, I will share my insights, knowledge, and practical tips to help you navigate the world of YouTube monetization and create a sustainable income stream from your channel.

Whether you're just starting out or have an existing YouTube channel, this book will provide you with a comprehensive guide on the opportunities and strategies for making money on YouTube. From understanding the YouTube Partner Program and sponsored content to affiliate marketing, merchandise sales, crowd-funding, and more, I will cover various monetization strategies that can work for different types of channels and niches. I will also provide advice on building a strong personal brand, engaging with your audience, and maintaining transparency and authenticity in your content. This book is not just about quick hacks or get-rich-quick schemes. It's about building a long-term, sustainable business on YouTube by leveraging the platform's features, understanding the audience, and creating valuable content that resonates with your viewers. It's about developing a strategic approach to monetization that aligns with your channel's goals and audience's interests. It's about understanding the ever-changing landscape of YouTube and adapting your strategies accordingly.

Throughout the book, I will share real-life examples, case studies, and practical tips to help you implement the strategies effectively. I will also provide guidance on navigating the challenges and pitfalls of YouTube monetization, such as dealing with copyright issues, managing sponsored content, and building a loyal fan-base. My aim is to empower you with the knowledge and tools needed to successfully monetize your YouTube channel and achieve your financial goals.

This book will serve as your comprehensive guide to making money on YouTube. Get ready to unlock the potential of YouTube and turn your passion into a profitable venture. Let's dive in and start your journey towards YouTube success.

Lecturer-1

YOUTUBE'S PARTNER PROGRAM (YPP)

YouTube's Partner Program (YPP) offers an opportunity for content creators to monetize their videos through advertisements. When you join the YPP and meet the eligibility requirements, ads may be displayed before or during your videos, or as display ads next to your video content. To start earning money through ads on YouTube, you need to create an AdSense account and link it to your YouTube channel. AdSense is Google's program that allows publishers, including YouTube creators, to display ads on their content and earn revenue when viewers interact with those ads.

Once you're approved for the YPP, ads may start appearing on your videos automatically. The types of ads that can be displayed include pre-roll ads, which play before your video starts; mid-roll ads, which appear during longer videos; and display ads, which are shown next to your video content. Earnings from ads on YouTube are based on various factors, such as the number of views, engagement, ad formats, ad targeting, and viewer demographics. The revenue is typically generated on a per-thousand-views (CPM) basis, where you earn a certain amount for every thousand views of ads on your videos. The CPM rates can vary greatly depending on the niche, audience demographics, and other factors. To optimize your earnings from ads, it's essential to create high-quality, engaging content that attracts viewers and encourages them to watch your videos for longer durations. Longer videos with more ad breaks may also generate more ad revenue, but it's important to strike a balance between ads and viewer experience to avoid excessive ads that may turn off your audience.

YouTube also provides tools and analytics to help you track your earnings and performance. You can access the YouTube Studio dashboard, where you can view your estimated revenue, ad performance, and other metrics. This data can help you understand which videos are performing well and make data-driven decisions to optimize your earnings. It's important to note that YouTube has strict policies and guidelines for ads, and it's crucial to comply with them to maintain your eligibility for the YPP. Violating YouTube's ad policies, such as posting content that is harmful, misleading, or violates copyright, can result in ads being disabled on your videos or even termination of your channel's monetization.

In addition to following YouTube's ad policies, it's also important to comply with Google's AdSense policies, which include requirements related to ad placement, ad format, and content quality. Violating AdSense policies can result in your AdSense account being disabled, which would affect your ability to earn money from ads on YouTube. It's also worth mentioning that earnings from ads on YouTube may not be substantial for all creators. Factors such as channel size, niche, audience engagement, and ad rates can greatly impact your earnings. Many creators rely on multiple revenue streams, such as sponsored content, merchandise sales, and crowd-funding, in addition to ads, to diversify their income and maximize their earnings.

In conclusion, the YouTube Partner Program offers an opportunity for content creators to monetize their videos through advertisements. By creating high-quality content, complying with YouTube's ad policies, and leveraging YouTube's tools and analytics, you can optimize your earnings from ads on YouTube. However, it's important to note that earnings from ads may vary depending on various factors, and it's essential to explore other revenue streams to diversify your income. With dedication, persistence, and strategic planning, you can turn your YouTube channel into a profitable venture and achieve success on the platform.

Lecturer- 2

SPONSORED CONTENT

Sponsored content, also known as brand partnerships or influencer marketing, is a popular way for content creators on YouTube to earn money by collaborating with brands. In sponsored content, creators promote products or services in their videos in exchange for payment from the brand.

Brands are often interested in partnering with YouTube creators because of their ability to reach and engage with specific target audiences. Creators with large and engaged audiences can provide valuable exposure and endorsement for a brand's products or services, leading to increased brand awareness and potential sales.

To get started with sponsored content, you can proactively reach out to brands that align with your channel's niche or content. Alternatively, brands may approach you if they are interested in partnering with your channel. It's important to choose brands that align with your values and content, as authenticity and trust are key factors in successful sponsored content. Once you've established a partnership with a brand, you will typically need to create content that integrates the brand's products or services seamlessly into your videos. This can be done through product reviews, demonstrations, testimonials, or other creative ways that align with your content and resonate with your audience. It's important to clearly disclose sponsored content in your videos as per YouTube's guidelines and regulations. You can do this by using terms such as "sponsored by," "in partnership with," or "paid promotion" in your video, description, or through on-screen graphics. Transparency is crucial to maintain the trust of your audience and comply with legal requirements.

The payment for sponsored content can vary depending on factors such as your channel size, audience engagement, and the brand's budget. Some brands may offer a fixed fee for a sponsored video, while others may offer a commission based on the number of views, clicks, or conversions generated by your content. It's important to negotiate and establish clear terms with the brand before creating the sponsored content. In addition to monetary compensation, brands may also provide free products, discounts, or other perks as part of the sponsorship agreement. It's essential to carefully review and understand the terms of the sponsorship agreement, including any exclusivity clauses or usage rights, before committing to the partnership.

To create successful sponsored content, it's crucial to maintain authenticity and align the content with your channel's tone and style. Your audience should feel that the sponsored content adds value and is in line with the overall theme of your channel. It's important to avoid overly promotional or forced content that may come across as inauthentic, as it can negatively impact your audience's trust and engagement. As with any other type of content, sponsored content should also comply with YouTube's community guidelines and policies. Avoid creating content that violates YouTube's rules, such as content that is harmful, misleading, or violates copyright. Violating YouTube's policies can result in your videos being removed or your channel being penalized, which can negatively impact your sponsored content opportunities and overall channel growth.

In conclusion, sponsored content is a viable way for YouTube creators to earn money by collaborating with brands. By creating authentic and value-added content that aligns with your channel's niche and audience, you can establish successful brand partnerships and generate revenue. However, it's important to disclose sponsored content transparently, negotiate clear terms with brands, and comply with YouTube's guidelines and policies to maintain the trust of your audience and ensure long-term success with sponsored content on YouTube.

Lecturer- 3

AFFILIATE MARKETING

Affiliate marketing is a popular way for YouTube creators to monetize their content and earn commissions by promoting products or services through affiliate links. Affiliate marketing involves partnering with brands or online marketplaces and earning a commission for every sale or referral made through the affiliate links.

One way to include affiliate links in your YouTube videos is by adding them to your video descriptions. You can provide links to products or services that you mention or review in your videos, and earn a commission when viewers click on those links and make a purchase. It's important to disclose that you're using affiliate links in your video descriptions to comply with FTC guidelines and maintain transparency with your audience.

YouTube also has its own built-in affiliate program called YouTube Affiliate Marketing. This program allows creators to add product recommendations to their videos through an affiliate feature called "Merch Shelf." Creators can promote products related to their content and earn a commission when viewers make purchases through their affiliate links on the Merch Shelf. To succeed with affiliate marketing on YouTube, it's important to choose products or services that are relevant to your audience and align with your channel's niche or content. Promoting products that you genuinely believe in and have used or tested can build trust with your audience and increase the likelihood of them making purchases through your affiliate links. It's also essential to create high-quality content that provides value to your viewers. Your videos should be engaging, informative, and authentic, with a clear call-to-action for viewers to click on your affiliate links. Avoid overly promotional or spammy content that can turn off your audience and negatively impact your affiliate marketing efforts.

In addition to video descriptions and YouTube Affiliate Marketing, you can also use other platforms, such as blogs or social media, to promote your affiliate links and drive traffic to your content on YouTube. Cross-promoting your content across different platforms can increase your reach and potential for earning commissions through affiliate marketing.

When it comes to earning commissions, the payment structure of affiliate marketing can vary depending on the affiliate program or network. Some programs offer a fixed commission per sale, while others may offer a percentage of the total purchase value. It's important to thoroughly review and understand the terms of the affiliate program you're participating in, including payment thresholds, commission rates, and payment methods. It's also important to disclose your use of affiliate links in your videos and descriptions, as required by FTC guidelines. You can do this by including clear and conspicuous disclosures such as "This video contains affiliate links" or "Affiliate links may be used in the description." Providing transparent disclosures helps maintain trust with your audience and ensures compliance with legal requirements.

As with any type of content, it's important to adhere to YouTube's community guidelines and policies when participating in affiliate marketing. Avoid promoting products or services that violate YouTube's rules, such as illegal or harmful items. Violating YouTube's policies can result in your videos being removed or your channel being penalized, which can negatively impact your affiliate marketing opportunities and overall channel growth.

In conclusion, affiliate marketing is a popular way for YouTube creators to earn commissions by promoting products or services through affiliate links. By choosing relevant products, creating high-quality content, and adhering to FTC guidelines and YouTube's policies, you can effectively monetize your content and earn commissions through affiliate marketing on YouTube. Remember to always provide transparent disclosures and maintain authenticity with your audience to build trust and ensure long-term success with affiliate marketing on YouTube.

Lecturer- 4

MERCHANDISE SALES

Selling branded merchandise is a popular way for YouTube creators to monetize their channel and engage with their audience. By creating and selling merchandise, such as t-shirts, mugs, or other products featuring your channel's logo or catchphrase, you can not only earn revenue but also promote your brand and build a loyal fan-base.

One of the key advantages of selling merchandise is that it allows you to leverage your channel's branding and identity. Your logo, catchphrase, or other unique elements of your channel can be incorporated into the design of your merchandise, making it exclusive to your channel and appealing to your dedicated audience. Merchandise serves as a tangible representation of your brand, and it can help foster a sense of community among your viewers.

Setting up an online store to sell merchandise can be relatively easy and cost-effective. There are various platforms, such as Shopify, Teespring, or Redbubble, that allow you to create and sell custom merchandise without the need for upfront inventory or production costs. These platforms typically handle the manufacturing, shipping, and customer service, leaving you with the task of designing and promoting your merchandise. To succeed with selling merchandise, it's important to create unique and appealing designs that resonate with your audience. Consider incorporating your channel's logo, catchphrase, or inside jokes into the design to make it exclusive to your channel. You can also collaborate with artists or designers to create custom artwork for your merchandise. High-quality designs that are visually appealing and aligned with your channel's branding can help drive sales and increase engagement with your audience.

Promoting your merchandise is crucial to its success. You can showcase your merchandise in your videos, social media posts, and other promotional materials. Create engaging content that highlights the features and benefits of your merchandise, and encourage your audience to support your channel by purchasing your merchandise. You can also offer special promotions, discounts, or limited-time offers to incentivize your viewers to make a purchase.

Engaging with your audience and fostering a sense of community is essential in the success of selling merchandise. Interact with your viewers through comments, social media, and other channels, and listen to their feedback and suggestions. Encourage them to share pictures of themselves wearing or using your merchandise, and showcase these user-generated content in your videos or social media posts. Building a loyal fan-base who are proud to support your channel through purchasing your merchandise can greatly impact your sales and brand loyalty. It's also important to consider factors such as pricing, quality, and customer service when selling merchandise. Set pricing that is reasonable and competitive, taking into account the production and shipping costs, as well as the value perceived by your audience. Ensure that the quality of your merchandise meets or exceeds your audience's expectations to maintain their trust and satisfaction. Providing excellent customer service, including timely shipping, easy returns, and responsive communication, can help build a positive reputation and encourage repeat purchases.

Keep in mind that selling merchandise requires careful planning and management. You'll need to keep track of inventory, monitor sales, and handle customer inquiries or issues. It's important to stay organized and responsive to ensure smooth operations and a positive customer experience.

In conclusion, selling branded merchandise is a lucrative opportunity for YouTube creators to monetize their channel and engage with their audience. By creating unique and appealing designs, promoting your merchandise, and fostering a sense of community, you can effectively generate revenue and build a loyal fanbase. Remember to prioritize quality, customer service, and effective management to ensure the success of your merchandise sales venture on YouTube.

Lecturer- 5

CROWD-FUNDING

Crowd-funding has become a popular way for YouTube creators to generate income by allowing their viewers to support their channel financially in exchange for exclusive content or perks. Platforms like Patreon or Kickstarter provide opportunities for creators to receive direct financial support from their audience, helping them to sustain and grow their channel.

Patreon, for example, is a subscription-based platform that allows creators to offer exclusive content or perks to their patrons in exchange for a recurring monthly payment. Creators can set up different tiers of membership, each with its own perks, such as early access to videos, behind-the-scenes content, or exclusive merchandise. Patrons, or supporters, get access to these exclusive offerings in return for their financial support. This model creates a direct connection between creators and their most dedicated fans, and it can provide a reliable source of income for creators.

Kickstarter, on the other hand, is a crowd-funding platform that allows creators to launch campaigns to fund specific projects, such as a new video series, a documentary, or a merchandise line. Creators set a funding goal and offer different levels of rewards to backers based on their contribution. If the campaign reaches its funding goal within a specified timeframe, the project is funded, and backers receive their rewards. This model allows creators to raise funds upfront for a specific project or venture, and it can be an effective way to generate the necessary funds to bring their creative ideas to life.

Crowd-funding can be a win-win for both creators and their audience. Creators receive direct financial support, which can help them cover production costs, invest in equipment, or hire additional staff to improve the quality of their content. In return, supporters get access to exclusive content or perks that are not available to regular viewers, creating a sense of exclusivity and appreciation for their support.

To succeed with crowd-funding, it's important to create compelling and enticing offerings for your audience. Consider what type of content or perks would be most appealing to your viewers and align with your channel's brand and niche. It's crucial to communicate the value of your offerings clearly and effectively to your audience to encourage them to support your campaign or become a patron.

Promotion is also key to a successful crowd-funding campaign. You'll need to spread the word about your campaign through your videos, social media, email lists, and other promotional channels. Create engaging content that showcases your campaign and encourages your audience to take action. Consider offering limited-time incentives or promotions to create a sense of urgency and encourage early support. Building a strong relationship with your audience is crucial in the success of crowd-funding. It's important to engage with your supporters and keep them updated on the progress of your campaign or project. Respond to their comments, messages, or questions, and express your gratitude for their support. Providing excellent customer service and maintaining transparent communication can help build trust and loyalty among your supporters, leading to long-term patronage or ongoing support.

It's also essential to set realistic goals and expectations for your crowd-funding campaign. Conduct thorough research to determine the costs involved in your project, including production, shipping, and other expenses, and set a funding goal that is achievable. Be transparent about how the funds will be used and provide regular updates on the progress of your project to keep your supporters informed. In conclusion, crowd-funding through platforms like Patreon or Kickstarter can be a viable way for YouTube creators to generate income and engage with their audience. By offering exclusive content or perks in exchange for financial support, creators can build a direct connection with their most dedicated fans and receive the necessary funds to support their creative projects. However, it requires careful planning, promotion, and relationship-building to succeed in crowd-funding, and creators should set realistic goals and expectations for their campaigns.

Lecturer- 6

DONATIONS

Another way for YouTube creators to generate income is through donations from their viewers. YouTube has a built-in feature called "Support" that allows creators to enable voluntary donations from their audience to support their channel.

The "Support" feature on YouTube allows viewers to make voluntary donations to a creator's channel. Viewers can choose to contribute a one-time donation or set up recurring donations on a monthly basis. Donations can be made directly on a creator's YouTube channel through the "Join" button or other donation options provided by YouTube. Enabling the "Support" feature can provide creators with an additional stream of income, as viewers who appreciate their content can choose to support them financially. Donations can help creators cover production costs, invest in better equipment, or simply provide them with extra income to sustain and improve their channel.

To encourage donations from viewers, creators can communicate the value of their content and the impact of viewer support. This can be done through video intros, outros, or verbal cues during the video. Creators can express their appreciation and gratitude towards their audience for considering making a donation, and highlight how the support can contribute to the quality and sustainability of their channel. Creators can also offer incentives or perks to viewers who make donations. For example, they can provide access to exclusive content, behind-the-scenes footage, or personalized shoutouts as a way to reward their supporters. These incentives can motivate viewers to make donations and feel valued for their support.

Promoting the "Support" feature on social media, in email newsletters, or through other promotional channels can also help raise awareness and encourage viewers to make donations. Creators can use their online presence to spread the word about their channel and the option to support them through donations. They can also express their gratitude towards their supporters publicly and recognize their contributions, which can encourage more viewers to follow suit.

It's important for creators to be transparent about how the donated funds will be used. Viewers are more likely to make donations if they know how their support will be utilized to benefit the creator's channel. Creators should communicate clearly about their plans and provide updates on how the funds are being used to build trust and maintain transparency with their audience.

However, it's important to note that donations may not be a reliable or sustainable source of income for all creators. It's crucial to have multiple revenue streams and not solely rely on donations as the primary source of income. Diversifying revenue streams through other methods such as ads, sponsorships, affiliate marketing, or merchandise sales can provide a more stable and consistent income for creators.

In conclusion, the "Support" feature on YouTube allows creators to enable voluntary donations from their audience as a way to generate income. By communicating the value of their content, offering incentives, promoting the option to support, and maintaining transparency with their audience, creators can encourage viewers to make donations to support their channel. However, it's important to diversify revenue streams and not solely rely on donations as the primary source of income.

Lecturer- 7

SPONSORED EVENTS

Hosting sponsored events, workshops, or meetups can be a lucrative way for YouTube creators to monetize their channel and engage with their audience in a more personal and interactive manner. By charging entry fees or collaborating with brands for sponsorship, creators can generate income while providing unique experiences for their viewers.

Sponsored events can come in various forms, such as workshops, meet-ups, or even larger-scale events like conferences or conventions. Creators can organize events related to their content niche or expertise, such as workshops on photography, cooking, fitness, or gaming, depending on their channel's theme and audience interests.

One way to monetize these events is by charging entry fees. Creators can set up ticket sales or registration fees for their events, and viewers who are interested in attending can purchase tickets or pay a fee to participate. The ticket sales can provide a direct source of income for the creator, covering the costs of organizing the event and generating a profit.

In addition to charging entry fees, creators can also collaborate with brands for sponsorship. Brands that are relevant to the creator's content niche can sponsor the event in exchange for promotional benefits, such as branding, product placement, or mentions during the event. This can provide an additional source of income for the creator and help offset the costs of organizing the event. When organizing sponsored events, it's important for creators to plan and execute the event professionally to ensure a successful experience for both the attendees and the sponsoring brands. This includes careful event planning, logistics management, and coordination with sponsors to fulfill their promotional requirements.

Promoting the sponsored event on the creator's YouTube channel, social media, email newsletters, and other online platforms can help generate awareness and drive ticket sales or registrations. Creators can create promotional content, such as teaser videos, blog posts, or social media posts, to highlight the event's value and encourage their audience to attend. During the event, creators should strive to deliver a high-quality experience for the attendees. This includes providing valuable content, engaging with the audience, and offering opportunities for networking, Q&A sessions, or meet-and-greets. Creators should also ensure that the sponsor's promotional requirements are met, such as displaying branding or showcasing sponsored products in a natural and authentic way.

After the event, creators can leverage the content generated from the event, such as event footage, testimonials, or testimonials, to create post-event content for their YouTube channel or other online platforms. This can help extend the event's reach and generate further engagement with the audience. It's important for creators to comply with relevant laws and regulations when organizing sponsored events, such as obtaining necessary permits or licenses, following advertising guidelines, and disclosing any sponsored content in accordance with YouTube's policies and local laws. This helps maintain transparency with the audience and builds trust with sponsors.

However, it's worth noting that organizing sponsored events can be time-consuming and require significant effort and resources. Creators should carefully consider their audience's interests, their own expertise, and the feasibility of hosting an event before committing to it. It's also important to have a backup plan and consider potential risks or challenges that may arise during the event planning and execution process.

In conclusion, hosting sponsored events, workshops, or meetups can be a profitable way for YouTube creators to monetize their channel and provide unique experiences for their audience. By charging entry fees or collaborating with brands for sponsorship, creators can generate income while delivering valuable content to their viewers. However, careful planning, professional execution, compliance with laws regulations, and consideration of potential risks are crucial for a successful event.

Lecturer- 8

BRAND PARTNERSHIPS

Brand partnerships are a popular way for YouTube creators to monetize their channel by collaborating with brands for long-term partnerships. These partnerships involve creating content that promotes a brand's products or services in exchange for ongoing payments or perks. Brand partnerships can be lucrative for creators, as they provide a consistent source of income and often offer additional benefits beyond monetary compensation. One of the key aspects of brand partnerships is selecting the right brands that align with the creator's content and audience. It's important for creators to choose brands that are relevant to their niche and resonate with their viewers. This ensures that the promoted content feels authentic and genuine, and resonates with the audience.

Once a brand partnership is established, creators can create content that showcases the brand's products or services in a creative and engaging way. This can include product reviews, tutorials, demonstrations, testimonials, or other types of content that highlight the brand's offerings. It's important for creators to maintain their own unique voice and style while integrating the brand's messaging into their content seamlessly.

In exchange for promoting the brand's products or services, creators typically receive ongoing payments or perks. Payments can be in the form of fixed fees, commissions, or revenue sharing arrangements, depending on the terms of the brand partnership. Perks may include free products, exclusive access, or other benefits that add value to the collaboration. Brand partnerships can provide creators with a consistent source of income, as they often involve long-term agreements. This can help creators to monetize their channel and generate revenue on an ongoing basis, beyond one-time payments from other monetization methods.

Furthermore, brand partnerships can offer additional benefits beyond monetary compensation. For example, creators may gain exposure to a wider audience through the brand's marketing efforts, which can help grow their channel and increase their viewership. Collaborating with reputable brands can also boost the creator's credibility and reputation, as it demonstrates endorsement and trust from established brands.

Building and maintaining strong relationships with brand partners is crucial for long-term success. This includes effective communication, meeting deliverables and deadlines, and being professional in all interactions. Creators should also be transparent with their audience about sponsored content and disclose any brand partnerships in accordance with YouTube's policies and local laws. Authenticity and transparency are essential in maintaining the trust of the audience. It's important for creators to carefully review and negotiate the terms of brand partnerships to ensure that they align with their goals and values. This includes considering the compensation structure, duration of the partnership, exclusivity clauses, and any other relevant terms. Seeking legal or professional advice may be beneficial in understanding the legal and financial implications of brand partnerships. However, it's important for creators to be mindful of the potential risks and challenges of brand partnerships. These may include conflicts of interest, potential negative impact on the audience's trust, and the need to balance promotional content with regular content to maintain authenticity. Creators should carefully consider the potential impact on their channel's content and audience before entering into brand partnerships.

In conclusion, brand partnerships can be a lucrative way for YouTube creators to monetize their channel by collaborating with brands for long-term partnerships. By creating content that promotes a brand's products or services in exchange for ongoing payments or perks, creators can generate consistent income and gain additional benefits such as exposure and credibility. However, it's important for creators to carefully select brand partnerships, negotiate favorable terms, and maintain authenticity and transparency with their audience to ensure long-term success.

Lecturer- 9

LICENSING YOUR CONTENT

L icensing your content is a strategy that allows YouTube creators to monetize their videos by selling the rights to third-party websites, TV networks, or other media outlets for use in their content. This can be a profitable way to generate revenue from your videos and expand your reach to wider audiences. The process of licensing your content involves granting permission to other entities to use your videos in their content in exchange for payment. This can include using your videos in TV shows, documentaries, advertisements, websites, or other media platforms. This can be especially beneficial if you have unique, high-quality, or exclusive content that is in demand by other media outlets.

One of the main advantages of licensing your content is the potential for higher payments compared to other monetization methods on YouTube. When your videos are used in other media outlets, you can negotiate licensing fees based on the value and exclusivity of your content. This can result in significant income for your channel, especially if your videos are widely popular or have a niche appeal. Additionally, licensing your content can also provide exposure to wider audiences. When your videos are used in other media platforms, they can reach new viewers who may not have discovered your content on YouTube. This can help you expand your reach and grow your audience, leading to increased visibility and potential for future opportunities. To license your content, you may need to work with third-party agencies, agents, or networks that specialize in content licensing. These entities can help you identify potential opportunities, negotiate licensing fees, and handle the legal and financial aspects of the licensing process. It's important to carefully review any contracts or agreements before entering into licensing deals, and seek legal or professional advice if needed to protect your rights and interests.

When licensing your content, it's crucial to maintain control over the usage and distribution of your videos. This may include specifying the platforms, regions, or timeframes for which the content can be used, and setting limitations on modifications or alterations to your videos. It's important to ensure that your content is used in a way that aligns with your brand and values, and that you retain ownership of your videos.

However, there are also potential challenges and risks associated with licensing your content. For instance, licensing your content may result in loss of exclusivity, as your videos may be used by other media outlets and become less unique or valuable. There is also a risk of copyright infringement, as other entities may use your content without proper authorization or attribution. Therefore, it's important to carefully vet potential licensing opportunities and ensure that proper contracts and agreements are in place to protect your content and rights.

In conclusion, licensing your content can be a profitable way for YouTube creators to monetize their videos by selling the rights to third-party websites, TV networks, or other media outlets. It offers the potential for higher payments and wider exposure to new audiences. However, it's important to carefully review and negotiate licensing deals, retain control over your content, and protect your rights to avoid potential challenges or risks. Licensing your content can be a valuable strategy for diversifying your revenue streams and maximizing the earning potential of your YouTube channel.

Lecturer- 10

CROWDSOURCING

Crowdsourcing is a popular strategy used by YouTube creators to raise funds for a particular project or video idea. By leveraging crowd-funding platforms such as Kickstarter, GoFundMe, or Patreon, creators can engage their audience and gather financial support to bring their creative vision to life.

Crowdsourcing involves reaching out to your audience, fans, and supporters to contribute funds towards a specific project or video idea. This can be anything from producing a documentary, creating a music video, launching a web series, or even starting a new channel. Creators typically set a funding goal and offer various incentives or rewards to encourage contributions from their community. One of the key benefits of crowdsourcing is that it allows creators to retain creative control and ownership over their projects. Unlike traditional funding methods where creators may have to rely on external sponsors or investors, crowdsourcing enables creators to gather support directly from their audience, without compromising their artistic vision or creative direction.

Crowdsourcing can also provide creators with the necessary financial resources to produce high-quality content that may not be feasible with their regular budget. This can include hiring professional equipment, talent, or resources to enhance the production value of their videos and deliver a more polished end result.

In addition to financial support, crowdsourcing also fosters a sense of community and engagement with the audience. Creators can involve their fans in the creative process, offer exclusive updates, behind-the-scenes content, or other perks as rewards for their contributions. This not only encourages financial support but also strengthens the relationship between the creator and their audience, fostering loyalty and support for future projects.

Crowdsourcing can also be a powerful marketing tool as it generates buzz and anticipation around the project. Creators can promote their crowd-funding campaign across various platforms, including social media, their YouTube channel, and other online communities. This can attract attention from new viewers, expand the reach of the project, and potentially garner media coverage or partnerships, further boosting the visibility and success of the campaign.

However, it's important to note that crowdsourcing is not without challenges. Crowd-funding campaigns require careful planning, preparation, and promotion to be successful. Creators need to create compelling campaigns, set realistic funding goals, and effectively communicate the value of their project to potential supporters. Crowd-funding platforms also charge fees or commissions on the funds raised, which creators need to take into account when planning their campaign.

Additionally, creators need to fulfill the promises and rewards offered to their supporters in a timely manner. This includes delivering the project as promised, providing updates, and fulfilling any physical rewards or perks offered. Meeting these obligations is crucial to maintaining the trust and loyalty of the audience and ensuring a positive crowd-funding experience.

In conclusion, crowdsourcing can be a viable strategy for YouTube creators to raise funds for a specific project or video idea. It offers the opportunity to retain creative control, engage with the audience, and gather the necessary financial resources to produce high-quality content. However, it requires careful planning, preparation, and promotion to be successful. Crowdsourcing can be a powerful tool for creators to bring their creative vision to life and connect with their audience on a deeper level.

Lecturer- 11

PRODUCT REVIEWS

Product reviews are a popular way for YouTube creators to earn money through sponsored reviews or affiliate links. By providing in-depth and unbiased reviews of products or services within their niche, creators can leverage their influence and expertise to monetize their content.

One common approach is through sponsored reviews, where creators collaborate with brands to review their products or services in exchange for payment. Brands may provide free products or compensation to the creator for their time and effort in creating the review. Sponsored reviews typically involve the creator using, testing, and evaluating the product or service, and sharing their honest opinions and experiences with their audience. To ensure transparency and maintain trust with their audience, it's essential for creators to disclose any sponsored content in their videos. This can be done through clear and prominent disclosures, such as verbal announcements or on-screen graphics, to inform viewers that the review is sponsored. Providing honest and unbiased reviews is crucial for maintaining the integrity of the content and preserving the trust of the audience. Another way to monetize product reviews is through affiliate marketing. Creators can include affiliate links in their video descriptions or use

YouTube's built-in affiliate program, YouTube Affiliate Marketing, to earn commissions when viewers make purchases through their links. When viewers click on these affiliate links and make a purchase, the creator earns a percentage of the sale as a commission. To be successful in affiliate marketing, creators need to choose relevant products or services that align with their niche and audience interests. It's important to provide genuine and honest reviews to maintain the trust of the audience. Creators should also disclose the use of affiliate links in their videos and descriptions to ensure transparency.

When creating product reviews, it's crucial for creators to focus on providing valuable and informative content. This includes thoroughly testing the product or service, highlighting its features and benefits, and sharing personal experiences or opinions. High-quality production values, engaging visuals, and clear audio are also important to create a professional and compelling review that resonates with the audience.

In addition to sponsored reviews and affiliate marketing, creators can also negotiate additional revenue streams through product reviews. This may include charging fees for dedicated review videos, integrating sponsored products into their regular content, or leveraging their review expertise to offer consultation or advisory services to brands. It's important for creators to establish a clear pricing structure, set boundaries, and negotiate contracts carefully when engaging in sponsored reviews or affiliate marketing. This includes specifying the scope of the review, the compensation, the timeline, and any other terms and conditions. Seeking legal or professional advice may also be necessary to ensure compliance with relevant laws and regulations, such as disclosure requirements or tax implications.

In conclusion, product reviews can be a lucrative way for YouTube creators to monetize their content through sponsored reviews or affiliate marketing. By providing valuable and unbiased reviews of products or services, creators can leverage their influence and expertise to earn money and provide valuable content to their audience. However, it's important to maintain transparency, provide honest opinions, and establish clear terms and conditions when engaging in product reviews to preserve the trust of the audience and ensure a successful and ethical monetization strategy.

Lecturer- 12

PATREON

Patreon is a popular crowd-funding platform that allows YouTube creators to earn money by offering exclusive content, behind-the-scenes access, or other perks to their Patreon subscribers in exchange for monthly payments. This model allows creators to establish a direct relationship with their most dedicated fans and monetize their content in a unique and personalized way.

One of the main advantages of using Patreon is that it provides a recurring revenue stream, as subscribers typically make monthly payments to support the creator's ongoing work. This can provide creators with a stable and predictable income, which can be particularly beneficial in an industry where revenue can be unpredictable, such as YouTube. To get started with Patreon, creators need to create an account on the platform and set up a page where they can showcase their content and perks. Creators can offer different tiers of membership, each with its own set of perks and pricing. For example, creators can offer a basic tier with access to exclusive content, a premium tier with additional perks like behind-the-scenes footage, and a higher-priced tier with even more exclusive perks or personalized interactions.

The key to success with Patreon is to offer compelling and valuable perks that incentivize viewers to become paying subscribers. These perks can include exclusive content, such as bonus videos, extended cuts, or early access to new videos. Creators can also offer behind-the-scenes content, such as bloopers, outtakes, or Q&A sessions with the creators. Other perks can include merchandise discounts, access to a private community or Discord group, personalized shoutouts, or even one-on-one consultations or mentoring sessions.

It's important for creators to be creative and tailor their perks to their audience's interests and preferences. Understanding the unique value proposition of their content and audience demographics can help creators determine the most appealing perks to offer. Regularly reviewing and updating the perks based on feedback from subscribers can also help keep the offerings fresh and relevant. In addition to offering perks, creators should also communicate the benefits of supporting their Patreon page to their audience through their YouTube videos, social media, and other promotional efforts. Clearly explaining the perks and the value they provide can help incentivize viewers to become patrons and support the creator's work.

Another aspect of Patreon is community engagement. Patreon provides a platform for creators to interact directly with their most dedicated fans, creating a sense of community and connection. This can include engaging with patrons through comments, responding to messages, hosting live Q&A sessions, or providing personalized shoutouts in videos. Building a strong community can foster loyalty and support among patrons, which can contribute to long-term success on Patreon. It's important for creators to set realistic pricing for their Patreon tiers. The pricing should be based on the perceived value of the perks offered and the financial situation of the target audience. Creators should also regularly review their pricing and adjust it as needed based on feedback, audience response, and overall business goals.

Lastly, creators should be transparent and authentic in their interactions with patrons. This includes regular updates on the progress of their work, sharing behind-the-scenes insights, and being responsive to feedback and suggestions from patrons. Building trust and maintaining open communication can help foster a strong relationship between the creator and their patrons, leading to ongoing support and loyalty.

In conclusion, Patreon can be a valuable revenue stream for YouTube creators, allowing them to monetize their content through offering exclusive perks and behind-the-scenes access to their most dedicated fans. By providing compelling perks, fostering community engagement, and maintaining transparency and authenticity, creators can build a successful Patreon page and generate recurring income to support their creative endeavors.

Lecturer-13

ONLINE COURSES

Creating and selling online courses can be a lucrative way for YouTube creators to monetize their expertise, skills, or niche. Online courses provide an opportunity for creators to share their knowledge, provide value to their audience, and generate revenue by charging for access to their educational content. To get started with creating and selling online courses, creators need to identify their area of expertise, skills, or niche that they want to teach. This can be anything from cooking, fitness, photography, music, language learning, or any other subject that aligns with their content and audience's interests. Creators should research the demand for their chosen topic and identify their target audience to ensure there is a viable market for their online course.

Once the topic and target audience are identified, creators can start planning and creating their course content. This can include creating video lessons, written materials, quizzes, assignments, or any other relevant content that provides value and helps learners achieve their desired outcomes. It's important for creators to ensure that their course content is well-organized, engaging, and provides a clear learning path for their students. Next, creators need to choose a platform to host and sell their online course. There are various online course platforms available, such as Teachable, Udemy, Thinkific, and many more, that provide the tools and infrastructure for creators to create, manage, and sell their courses. Creators should research and compare different platforms to choose the one that best fits their needs in terms of features, pricing, and ease of use. Once the course is created and uploaded to the chosen platform, creators can set the pricing for their course. It's important to consider the perceived value of the course content, the target audience's affordability, and the competitive landscape when determining the course price. Creators should also consider offering promotional discounts or early-bird pricing to incentivize early sign-ups and generate initial traction.

To promote the online course, creators can leverage their existing YouTube channel and social media presence to create awareness and generate interest. This can include creating promotional videos, teasers, or trailers for the course, mentioning it in their YouTube videos, and sharing about it on their social media accounts. Additionally, creators can collaborate with other influencers or affiliates to promote their course to a wider audience.

Customer support and engagement are crucial in the success of an online course. Creators should be responsive to student inquiries, provide timely feedback on assignments or quizzes, and actively engage with students to create a positive learning experience. This can lead to positive reviews, testimonials, and word-of-mouth marketing, which can help attract more students to the course. Another potential revenue stream from online courses is through upselling or cross-selling. Once students complete one course, creators can offer them additional courses, advanced modules, or supplementary materials to further their learning journey. This can help increase the lifetime value of each student and generate additional revenue. Creators should also continuously update and improve their course content based on feedback, student performance, and market trends. Keeping the course content up-to-date and relevant can help maintain student engagement and satisfaction, and attract new students over time.

Lastly, creators should ensure that they comply with applicable laws and regulations, such as copyright, intellectual property, data protection, and consumer rights, when creating and selling online courses. This includes properly citing and attributing any third-party content used in the course, obtaining necessary permissions or licenses, and providing clear terms and conditions to students.

In conclusion, creating and selling online courses can be a profitable way for YouTube creators to monetize their expertise, skills, or niche. By identifying a viable topic, creating high-quality course content, choosing a suitable platform, promoting the course, providing excellent customer support, and continuously improving the content, creators can generate revenue from online courses and provide value to their audience in an educational and engaging way.

Lecturer- 14

PUBLIC SPEAKING

Leveraging public speaking engagements can be a lucrative way for YouTube creators to monetize their expertise and gain exposure outside of their online platform. By showcasing their skills and knowledge on their YouTube channel, creators can establish themselves as experts in their niche and secure paid speaking engagements at events or conferences. To get started with public speaking, creators need to identify the events or conferences that align with their niche or target audience. This can be industry-specific conferences, seminars, workshops, or any other relevant events where their expertise can provide value. Creators should research and identify the events that are relevant to their niche, have a large audience, and offer paid speaking opportunities.

Once the target events are identified, creators can start promoting their expertise on their YouTube channel. This can include creating videos that demonstrate their knowledge, skills, and expertise in their niche. They can also showcase their previous speaking engagements or presentations to establish credibility and showcase their speaking abilities. Creators can use their YouTube channel to share valuable insights, tips, and advice related to their niche, and position themselves as thought leaders in their field. Creators should also create a speaker profile or media kit that includes their bio, credentials, speaking topics, and contact information. This can be shared on their YouTube channel, website, or social media accounts to make it easy for event organizers to learn about their expertise and reach out for potential speaking opportunities. To secure paid speaking engagements, creators can proactively reach out to event organizers, conference planners, or industry associations to express their interest in speaking at their events. They can provide their speaker profile or media kit and highlight the value they can bring to the event through their expertise and engaging speaking style. Creators should customize their pitch based on the specific event and audience, and highlight how their content aligns with the event's theme or objectives.

In addition to proactive outreach, creators can also leverage their existing network and industry connections to secure speaking engagements. They can collaborate with other influencers or professionals in their niche, participate in panel discussions, or join industry associations or networking groups to expand their reach and visibility in their industry. Word-of-mouth marketing and referrals from industry peers can also lead to paid speaking opportunities. When negotiating speaking fees, creators should consider factors such as their experience, expertise, audience size, and the event's budget. It's important to have a clear understanding of the event's expectations, including the speaking duration, format, and any additional requirements or expenses. Creators should also be prepared to provide a professional and engaging presentation, and deliver value to the event attendees through their content and delivery. During the speaking engagement, creators should be prepared to engage with the audience, provide value, and deliver a memorable presentation. They should also be open to networking opportunities, connecting with event attendees, and building relationships that can potentially lead to future speaking engagements or collaborations.

After the speaking engagement, creators should follow up with event organizers and express gratitude for the opportunity. They can also request feedback on their presentation and ask for testimonials or references that can be used for future promotional purposes. It's important to maintain a professional and positive relationship with event organizers, as they can be valuable contacts for future speaking engagements.

In conclusion, public speaking can be a profitable way for YouTube creators to monetize their expertise and gain exposure outside of their online platform. By showcasing their skills and knowledge on their YouTube channel, reaching out to event organizers, and delivering engaging presentations, creators can secure paid speaking engagements at events or conferences. It's important to have a professional speaker profile, negotiate fair speaking fees, deliver high-quality presentations, and maintain positive relationships with event organizers to build a successful public speaking career.

Lecturer-15

FREELANCE SERVICES

Offering freelance services can be a viable way for YouTube creators to monetize their skills and expertise by providing valuable services to their viewers in exchange for payment. Creators can leverage their YouTube channel to showcase their abilities and attract clients who are in need of services such as video editing, graphic design, consulting, and more. To get started with offering freelance services, creators should identify their core strengths and skills that are in demand within their niche or target audience. This could include video editing, animation, graphic design, copywriting, social media management, consulting, or any other relevant services that align with their expertise and audience needs.

Once the services are identified, creators can create a dedicated section on their YouTube channel or website that showcases the services they offer, along with pricing, packages, and contact information. They can also create sample portfolios or demonstrate their work through videos to provide potential clients with a clear understanding of the quality and value they can offer. Creators should also proactively promote their freelance services on their YouTube channel through video content, social media, and other marketing channels. They can create videos that highlight their skills and expertise, provide insights and tips related to their services, and share testimonials from satisfied clients. They can also use their existing audience and community on YouTube to spread the word about their services and ask for referrals. Additionally, creators can leverage their existing network and industry connections to find clients for their freelance services. They can reach out to fellow You-Tubers, industry influencers, or professionals in their niche and offer their services. Collaborations with other creators or businesses can also lead to referrals and potential clients for their freelance services.

When setting pricing for their freelance services, creators should consider factors such as their experience, expertise, market demand, and the complexity of the services. It's important to set fair and competitive prices that reflect the value they provide, while also considering the budget of their potential clients. They can offer different packages or pricing tiers to cater to different budgets or requirements. When working with clients, creators should maintain clear communication, establish clear expectations, and provide professional and timely service. They should deliver their services according to the agreed-upon timelines, and be responsive to client feedback and revisions. Building a reputation for excellent customer service and quality work can lead to repeat business and positive word-of-mouth marketing.

Creators should also establish clear payment terms and policies, such as upfront payments, milestones, or invoices. It's important to have a clear understanding of payment expectations and communicate them to clients upfront to avoid any misunderstandings or payment delays. In addition to one-time freelance services, creators can also consider offering retainer or ongoing service packages to provide recurring revenue streams. This can include monthly retainer packages for ongoing video editing, social media management, or consulting services. Retainer packages can provide a stable source of income and long-term client relationships. As with any business venture, creators should also be mindful of legal considerations, such as contracts, intellectual property rights, and tax obligations. It's important to have clear contracts or agreements in place to protect both parties' interests and to comply with relevant laws and regulations.

In conclusion, offering freelance services can be a profitable way for YouTube creators to monetize their skills and expertise by providing valuable services to their viewers. By showcasing their services on their YouTube channel, promoting their services through various marketing channels, maintaining excellent customer service, and establishing fair pricing and payment policies, creators can build a successful freelance services business. It's important to be proactive in promoting their services, building a strong reputation, and complying with legal considerations to ensure a sustainable and profitable freelance services venture.

Lecturer-16

CROWD-FUNDED PRODUCTIONS

C rowd-funding platforms can provide a creative and effective way for YouTube creators to fund larger-scale productions, such as short films, documentaries, or music videos. Crowd-funded productions allow creators to raise funds from their viewers and fans directly, empowering them to bring their creative visions to life without relying solely on traditional funding sources.

To start a crowd-funded production, creators can identify the project they want to fund and set a realistic fundraising goal. This could include a short film, a documentary on a particular topic, or a music video for their original song. They can then choose a crowd-funding platform that aligns with their project and audience, such as Kickstarter, Indiegogo, or Patreon. Once the crowd-funding campaign is set up, creators should create a compelling pitch that clearly communicates their project's vision, goals, and why it's worth supporting. This can be done through a video, written description, images, and other creative elements. They should also clearly outline the rewards or perks backers will receive for their support, such as early access to the finished production, exclusive behind-the-scenes content, or limited edition merchandise.

Creators should leverage their existing YouTube channel and social media presence to promote their crowd-funding campaign. They can create videos that showcase their project, share the campaign link in video descriptions, and create engaging social media posts to spread the word. They can also collaborate with other You-Tubers, industry influencers, or relevant communities to amplify their campaign's reach.

It's crucial for creators to engage with their backers and potential backers throughout the campaign by providing regular updates on the progress of the project, expressing gratitude, and answering questions. This helps build trust and keeps backers excited and invested in the project. In addition to the initial fundraising goal, creators can also set stretch goals to incentivize further contributions and keep the momentum going. Stretch goals can include additional features, enhancements, or expansions of the project, which can generate more excitement and motivate backers to increase their support.

Once the crowd-funding campaign reaches its goal, creators should deliver on their promises by creating and delivering the production as planned. They should also fulfill the rewards or perks promised to backers in a timely manner, as this is a crucial part of maintaining trust and building a loyal community. Crowd-funded productions can also provide opportunities for creators to collaborate with other professionals in the industry, such as actors, directors, cinematographers, or musicians. This can enhance the production value and quality of the final product, and also create valuable networking and partnership opportunities for the creator. Creators should also be mindful of legal considerations when running a crowd-funded production, such as taxes, contracts, and intellectual property rights. It's important to have clear contracts or agreements in place with collaborators, and to comply with relevant laws and regulations to protect both the creator's and the backers' interests. Crowd-funding campaigns can also serve as a way to gauge market demand and gather feedback from the audience. Creators can use the campaign as a way to test the viability of their project, gather feedback from backers, and refine their ideas before bringing the final production to a wider audience.

In conclusion, crowd-funded productions can be a viable way for YouTube creators to fund larger-scale projects, such as short films, documentaries, or music videos. By leveraging their existing audience, promoting their campaign through various channels, engaging with backers, and delivering on promises, creators can successfully bring their creative visions to life. Crowd-funding campaigns also provide opportunities for collaboration, feedback, and market validation, while being mindful of legal considerations. With careful planning, execution, and community engagement, crowd-funded productions can be a successful and rewarding way for YouTube creators to create impactful and high-quality productions.

Lecturer-17

BRAND AMBASSADORSHIPS

Brand ambassadorships can be a lucrative way for YouTube creators to monetize their channel by partnering with companies and promoting their products or services across their videos and social media platforms. As a brand ambassador, creators become the face of a brand and actively endorse their offerings to their audience in exchange for payment.

To become a brand ambassador, creators should identify brands that align with their niche, content, and audience. They can research companies that offer products or services relevant to their channel, and reach out to them with a compelling pitch showcasing the value they can provide as a brand ambassador. Alternatively, brands may also approach creators directly for potential partnership opportunities. Once a brand ambassadorship is established, creators should ensure that they are transparent with their audience about their partnership. This includes disclosing any paid partnerships or sponsored content in compliance with relevant advertising regulations, such as the UK Advertising Standards Authority (ASA) guidelines. Transparency and authenticity are key in maintaining the trust of the audience and building a long-term relationship with the brand. As a brand ambassador, creators should genuinely believe in the products or services they are endorsing, and create high-quality, engaging content that showcases the brand in an authentic and appealing way. This can include product reviews, tutorials, testimonials, or other creative formats that align with the creator's content style and audience preferences. Creators should also leverage their social media platforms, such as Instagram, Twitter, or Facebook, to promote the brand and its offerings. This can include sharing sponsored content, behind-the-scenes glimpses, or exclusive promotions. Social media can be a powerful tool to expand the reach of the brand's message and engage with the audience in a more personal and interactive manner. In addition to creating sponsored content, creators should also engage with the brand's community and respond to comments, messages, and inquiries from the audience. This helps to build a strong relationship with the brand's audience and creates a positive impression of the brand and the creator.

It's important for creators to negotiate and set clear expectations with the brand regarding the scope of work, deliverables, payment terms, and other contractual details. This includes the duration of the brand ambassadorship, the number of sponsored content pieces, the exclusivity of the partnership, and the payment structure. Creators should carefully review and understand the terms of the agreement and seek legal advice if needed to protect their interests. Brand ambassadorships can also provide opportunities for creators to collaborate with the brand on other projects, such as product development, events, or campaigns. This can enhance the creator's exposure, expertise, and credibility, and create valuable networking and partnership opportunities. Creators should also track and report the performance of their sponsored content to the brand, providing data and insights on metrics such as views, engagement, conversions, and audience demographics. This helps the brand to assess the effectiveness of the partnership and make data-driven decisions for future collaborations. It's crucial for creators to be selective and mindful of the brands they choose to partner with, ensuring that the brand's values, mission, and offerings align with their own content and audience. Authenticity and transparency are key in maintaining the trust of the audience and building a strong and genuine relationship with the brand.

In conclusion, brand ambassadorships can be a lucrative way for YouTube creators to monetize their channel by partnering with companies and promoting their products or services. By creating high-quality, engaging, and authentic content, leveraging social media, negotiating clear expectations, and maintaining transparency with their audience, creators can successfully establish brand partnerships and generate income from their YouTube channel. Brand ambassadorships also provide opportunities for collaboration, networking, and professional growth, while being mindful of maintaining authenticity and integrity in the content creation process. With careful planning, execution, and brand alignment, brand ambassadorships can be a win-win partnership for both creators and brands alike.

Lecturer-18

FAN MEMBERSHIPS

Fan memberships, also known as the "Memberships" feature on YouTube, can be a valuable way for creators to monetize their channel by offering exclusive perks and content to their most dedicated fans in exchange for a recurring monthly payment. This feature enables creators to cultivate a loyal community of supporters and provide them with additional value beyond their regular content. To enable the Memberships feature, creators need to meet certain requirements, such as having at least 30,000 subscribers, being a part of the YouTube Partner Program, and having no Community Guidelines or copyright strikes. Once eligible, creators can set up different membership tiers with varying perks and pricing, such as access to exclusive videos, behind-the-scenes content, merchandise discounts, custom emojis, or shout-outs.

Creating compelling and exclusive content is key to enticing viewers to become paying members. Creators should carefully consider the perks they offer and ensure they are unique, valuable, and align with their audience's interests. It's important to communicate the benefits of being a member clearly in their videos, social media, and other promotional materials to encourage viewers to join. In addition to exclusive content, creators should also actively engage with their members to foster a sense of community and belonging. This can include responding to member comments, hosting members-only live streams, polls, or Q&A sessions, and acknowledging their support in a special way. This personal interaction can deepen the connection between creators and their fans and encourage more viewers to become paying members.

Promoting the Memberships feature on YouTube is essential to drive awareness and encourage viewers to join. Creators can mention it in their videos, create dedicated promotional content, pin membership-related comments, or use end screens and annotations to direct viewers to their membership page. It's important to consistently remind viewers of the benefits of becoming a member and make it easy for them to join. Creators should also consider offering incentives or limited-time promotions to entice viewers to become members. This can include special discounts, bonuses, or perks for early joiners or for those who commit to a longer membership period. Limited-time offers can create a sense of urgency and encourage viewers to take action. Regularly reviewing and optimizing the membership perks and pricing is crucial to keep the offering fresh and appealing to viewers. Creators should gather feedback from their members, monitor the performance of their perks, and make adjustments accordingly. This can include adding new perks, removing underperforming perks, or adjusting the pricing based on the value provided. Creators should also maintain transparency with their audience and clearly communicate how the membership revenue is used to support their content creation. This can include investments in equipment, production, or hiring additional team members. Being transparent about the use of the membership revenue helps to build trust with the audience and ensures they understand the value they are receiving in exchange for their support. Managing the technical aspects of the Memberships feature, such as setting up payment processing, tracking memberships, and fulfilling perks, requires careful attention. Creators should familiarize themselves with the features and tools available in the YouTube Studio and ensure they are complying with YouTube's policies and guidelines. Creators should also consider diversifying their revenue streams and not solely relying on fan memberships. YouTube's monetization policies and algorithms can change, and it's important to have multiple income sources to mitigate risks. This can include other monetization methods, such as advertising revenue, merchandise sales, affiliate marketing, or sponsored content.

In conclusion, fan memberships on YouTube can be a valuable way for creators to monetize their channel and cultivate a loyal community of supporters. By offering exclusive perks, engaging with members, promoting the feature, optimizing perks and pricing, and maintaining transparency with their audience, creators can successfully generate income from their fan memberships. It's important to diversify revenue streams and consistently provide value to members to ensure their continued support. With careful planning, execution

Lecturer-19

SELLING YOUR CHANNEL

Selling your YouTube channel can be a lucrative way to monetize your hard work and dedication in building a substantial following. When a YouTube channel has a significant audience and engagement, it can be attractive to potential buyers who are looking for an established online presence. However, selling a YouTube channel requires careful consideration and understanding of the platform's policies and guidelines. Before selling your YouTube channel, it's crucial to ensure that you comply with YouTube's terms of service and community guidelines. Any violations, such as copyright infringements, misleading content, or spamming, can result in the termination of your channel and may affect its value to potential buyers. It's important to review your channel's content, metadata, and engagement to ensure that it aligns with YouTube's policies.

When it comes to finding potential buyers, there are different options available. You can directly reach out to interested parties or explore online marketplaces or platforms that facilitate the buying and selling of YouTube channels. It's important to thoroughly vet potential buyers and ensure that they have a genuine interest in your channel and its content. It's also essential to have a clear agreement in place that outlines the terms and conditions of the sale, including the transfer of ownership and any ongoing responsibilities or liabilities. The value of your YouTube channel depends on various factors, such as the number of subscribers, engagement rate, niche, content quality, monetization potential, and overall brand value. Channels with a large and engaged audience are generally more valuable to potential buyers. It's important to provide accurate and verifiable data about your channel's performance, including statistics on subscribers, views, watch time, and revenue, to establish its value.

It's also essential to consider the potential risks and challenges associated with selling a YouTube channel. YouTube's policies and algorithms are subject to change, and the new owner may face challenges in maintaining the channel's performance or adapting to future updates. Additionally, the audience may have a personal connection with the original creator, and a change in ownership may impact their engagement and loyalty. It's important to be transparent with the potential buyer about any potential risks and challenges they may face after acquiring the channel.

When selling your YouTube channel, it's important to protect your personal information and account credentials. Ensure that you use secure and reputable platforms or methods for communication and transfer of ownership. Avoid sharing sensitive information, such as passwords or payment details, unless necessary and with proper safeguards in place. It's also important to consider the impact of selling your YouTube channel on your personal brand and online presence. If you have built a personal brand around your YouTube channel, selling it may affect your overall brand image and reputation. It's crucial to carefully consider the implications and weigh the pros and cons before making a decision. Lastly, it's important to have a plan for what you will do after selling your YouTube channel. Selling a successful YouTube channel can provide a financial windfall, but it also means letting go of something you have built and nurtured. Consider your future goals, interests, and passions, and have a plan in place for how you will move forward after the sale.

In conclusion, selling a YouTube channel can be a viable way to monetize your online presence if you have a substantial following and engagement. However, it requires careful consideration of YouTube's policies, finding potential buyers, establishing the value of your channel, managing risks and challenges, protecting your personal information, and planning for the future. Selling a YouTube channel is a significant decision, and it's important to weigh the pros and cons and make an informed decision that aligns with your long-term goals and interests.

CONCLUSION

In conclusion, there are numerous ways to monetize your YouTube channel and earn money from your content. From ads and sponsored content to affiliate marketing and merchandise sales, YouTube offers a variety of revenue-generating opportunities for content creators with substantial followings.

The YouTube Partner Program is a popular choice for many creators, as it allows them to earn money through advertisements that play before or during their videos, or as display ads next to their video content. By meeting YouTube's requirements for monetization, such as reaching a certain number of subscribers and watch hours, creators can start earning revenue from their videos through the Partner Program.

Sponsored content is another common method of monetization, where creators collaborate with brands and promote their products or services in their videos in exchange for payment. This can include product reviews, sponsored integrations, or sponsored mentions. Affiliate marketing is also popular, as creators can include affiliate links in their video descriptions or use YouTube's built-in affiliate program to earn commissions when viewers make purchases through their links.

Merchandise sales offer an opportunity for creators to sell branded merchandise, such as t-shirts, mugs, or other products featuring their channel's logo or catchphrase. This can be a lucrative way to monetize a dedicated fan base that is interested in supporting the creator by purchasing merchandise.

Crowd-funding is another option for creators to raise funds for their channel or specific projects. Platforms like Patreon or Kick starter allow viewers to support their favorite creators financially in exchange for exclusive content or perks. This can include behind-the-scenes access, early access to videos, or personalized content.

Donations are another way to earn money from your YouTube channel, as viewers can make voluntary donations through the "Support" feature on YouTube. This allows viewers to support their favorite creators directly and can be a source of additional income for creators.

Brand partnerships can offer long-term revenue opportunities, as creators can collaborate with brands for ongoing payments or perks in exchange for creating content around their products or services. This can include sponsored videos, sponsored live streams, or other promotional activities.

Licensing your content to third-party websites, TV networks, or other media outlets can also generate revenue for your channel. If you have unique or high-quality content, you may be able to sell the rights to your videos for use in other media productions. In addition to these options, creators can also offer online courses related to their niche, expertise, or skills, sell freelance services to their viewers, host sponsored events or workshops, or even become brand ambassadors for companies. Fan memberships and sponsored live streams are also popular ways to engage with your audience in real-time and earn money through donations or sponsorships.

Finally, if you have built a substantial following on your YouTube channel, you may have the option to sell your channel to interested buyers who are willing to pay for an established YouTube presence. This can be a significant source of revenue, especially for creators who have put in years of hard work to build their channel's audience.

In conclusion, YouTube offers a wide range of monetization options for content creators to earn money from their channels. By exploring different revenue streams, creators can diversify their income and generate revenue from multiple sources. It's important to consider your niche, audience, and content when choosing the right monetization methods for your channel, and to comply with YouTube's guidelines and policies to ensure a successful and sustainable monetization strategy. With dedication, creativity, and strategic planning, you can turn your YouTube channel into a profitable venture and make a living doing what you love.